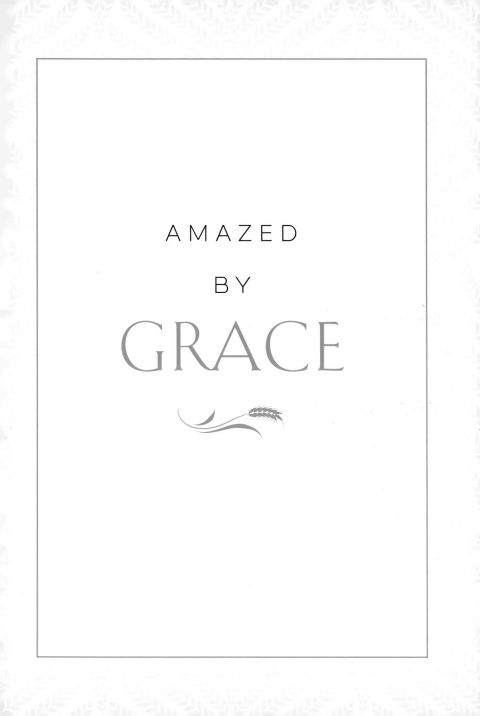

AMAZED

BY

GRACE

Library of Congress Cataloging-in-Publication Data

Dew, Sheri L., author.
  Amazed by grace / Sheri Dew.
    pages cm
  Includes bibliographical references.
  ISBN 978-1-62972-039-5 (hardbound : alk. paper)
1. Atonement—The Church of Jesus Christ of Latter-day Saints. 2. Grace (Theology) 3. The Church of Jesus Christ of Latter-day Saints—Doctrines. 4. Mormon Church—Doctrines. I. Title.
  BX8643.A85D49 2015
  234—dc23   2014046490

Printed in the United States of America
Publishers Printing, Salt Lake City, UT

10 9 8 7 6 5 4 3 2 1

AMAZED

BY

GRACE

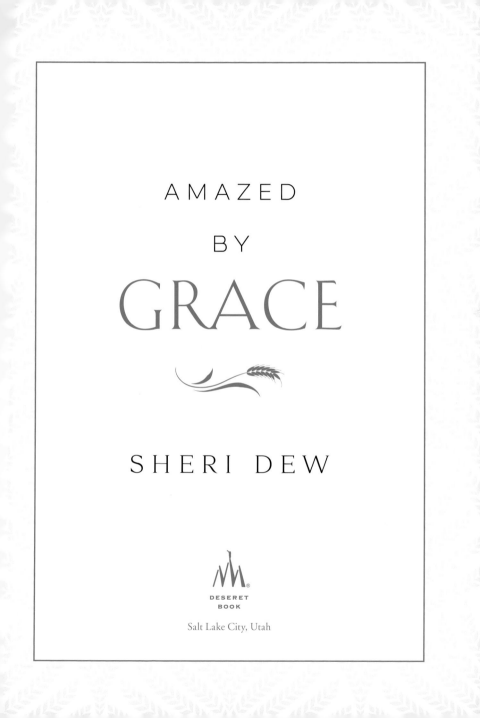

SHERI DEW

DESERET BOOK

Salt Lake City, Utah

I was once invited to speak at the BYU Women's Conference on the subject of grace and was overwhelmed at the prospect of attempting to teach and convey the majesty of doctrine so central to the Atonement. A dear friend who knew I was wrestling with the assignment sent me an email that I'm sure she meant to be helpful. Her email read: "Here is what I hope you cover in your talk. What is grace? How do I gain access to it? What difference does grace make in my life? Can it help me with loneliness, with overeating, with bad relationships, with weaknesses and temptations, with insecurity, with heartache and stress? Can it help me with my family? Is grace always present, or do I have to do something to get it? Is it a feeling? How can I tell when grace is helping me? Okay, those are the questions I want you to answer."

My response to her was a one-liner: "Are you sure that's *all* you want to know?"

Her email led me to ask other friends what they wanted to understand about grace. One of them said, "To tell you the truth, TV evangelists have wrecked that word for me. I almost feel disloyal to the restored gospel even talking about grace. I mean, do *we* believe in grace?"

I then asked a longtime friend who was serving as a stake Relief Society president to ask her presidency what they wished the women in their stake understood about grace. This presidency is a spectacular quartet of women who have logged decades of service. And yet, after a long discussion, they said, "We don't think we know enough about grace to even know what to ask."

The disturbing and even tragic irony in all of these comments is that *the central, most*

THE KEY TO UNLOCKING

the power of

His covenant sons

and daughters

— IS IN —

His covenant sons'

and daughters'

learning to unlock

the power of

JESUS CHRIST.

compelling, most life-changing message of all time is that

JESUS CHRIST HAS ALREADY TRIUMPHED OVER SIN, DEATH, HELL, TEMPTATION, AND EVERY KIND OF MISERY.

And yet, perhaps it shouldn't surprise us that imperfect people—as we all are—struggle to comprehend the Savior's perfect love. Surely there is *nothing* our Father is more eager for us to understand than that—which includes the breathtaking scope of the Atonement of His Son and the power the Atonement makes available to us. *Because the key to unlocking the power of His covenant sons and daughters is in His covenant sons' and daughters' learning to unlock the power of Jesus Christ.*

With this truth in mind, let's consider four of my friend's questions. First, what is grace? Second, what difference can grace make in our lives? Third, how *does* the Savior make His power available to us? And fourth, what must *we* do to gain access to that power?

WHAT IS GRACE?

My father had many virtues. He served faithfully in the Church his entire life. I doubt he ever missed home teaching in sixty years, though he had to drive a hundred miles every month to do it, and he served diligently in numerous leadership capacities. My earliest testimony of priesthood power came from him, and I could always feel the presence of the Spirit when he gave me a father's blessing. After his death, we heard story after story about his quiet generosity. And my father's word was gold. Everyone who knew him knew that if Charles Dew said he would do something, they could take that commitment to the bank. But my dad had an Achilles heel—a temper he never conquered. We knew he loved us, but we often bore the brunt of his anger. And anger *always* complicates relationships.

One afternoon a few days before he died, I was sitting at his bedside as he slept. Suddenly I found myself asking the Lord to forgive him for years of angry outbursts. I wasn't praying that *I* could forgive him; I was praying for his eternal well-being.

As I prayed, something unexplainable happened to me. In an instant, I felt decades of hurt simply fall away.

The feeling was spiritual but it was also tangible—even physical. I could *remember* my dad's anger, but I couldn't *feel* any of the related pain or disappointment. It was gone. It was beauty for ashes.[1] It was sweet.

That is grace. The amazing power of grace. No earthly remedy could have done for me what the Savior did in that moment. It was the redeeming power of Jesus Christ that prompted me to pray for my father and even gave me the words to say, and it was His healing power that healed a lifetime of wounds.

My experience is neither unique nor rare. On September 11, 2001, a dear friend and colleague of mine was headed to the World Trade Center via subway from his apartment in Brooklyn. There he was to catch the PATH train running under the Hudson River to his office in Jersey City. At the subway stop just before the World Trade Center, the conductor advised the passengers to get off the subway, as smoke was filling the World Trade Center subway station. My friend complied and surfaced onto the street just in time to see one tower in flames and United Flight 175 crash into the other tower. The explosion was deafening, and as airplane parts and other large chunks of debris began to fall from the sky, a police officer tackled him to shield him from danger. The horrors of that day have been well documented, and my friend was right in the middle of it. In his words: "I was a block away when Tower 2 collapsed. It was terrifying, loud, and I found myself running from a massive debris cloud that filled lower Manhattan. The debris cloud consumed us. Everything went dark."

After several hours, he made it home—all the while worrying about his pregnant wife, who was trying to make her way home on foot from midtown Manhattan. But the impact of what he'd seen and felt—along with the fact that some of his friends had died in the tragedy—was devastating, and the effect of those graphically horrible events lingered with him and even grew in intensity in his heart and mind. "A sense of rage and anger possessed me like never before," he said. "I knew forgiveness would never be an option for the people responsible for this, and a dark seed was planted in my heart."

My friend's smoldering sense of darkness stretched from months to years. He tried to put on a good face to family and friends, but inside he wrestled with everything from survivor's guilt ("Why did I live when some of my dear friends died?") to rage to hatred for the perpetrators. He put on weight. His relationships changed. His wife watched her husband's native cheery disposition become more surly. One day she acted on a prompting to buy him a road bike, and he began to ride his new bike with a vengeance. For months he rode and rode and rode—almost as though he was trying to pedal the anger and the hurt out of him. As it turned out, he was a natural-born cyclist, good enough to be competitive in races. Cycling grew in importance in his life. Then one day while on a training ride he had an experience unlike anything he had experienced before. Again, in his words:

"A VOICE CAME INTO MY MIND SO CLEARLY THAT IT WAS ALMOST AS THOUGH SOMEONE WAS RIDING BESIDE ME.

"The voice said, 'Why are you carrying all of this extra weight? You need to let it go. I already paid the price for their sins, your sins, all sins. I have already carried that burden. I did it thousands of years ago. You need to let it go.' Tears began to stream down my face, and I felt peace for the first time in several years. Even more, I felt an overwhelming sense of love for God's children—including those who had attacked us. The bitterness was simply gone."

The scriptures explain what my friend experienced on his bike and what I experienced at my father's bedside. In Lehi's vision of the tree of life, most of those he saw never even entered the "covenant path,"[2] or they got lost somewhere along the way.[3] But one group *held fast* to the iron rod, pressed forward to the tree and partook of the fruit, and *heeded not* those who mocked them.[4] The fruit made them happy and filled their souls with "exceedingly great joy."[5] It was "sweet above all that is sweet."[6]

The fruit that Nephi said was "*most* desirable above all things"[7] is the Atonement, which is *the most tangible evidence* of the Lord's incomprehensible love for us.

GRACE IS THE POWER THAT FLOWS
FROM THE ATONEMENT.

It is what the Savior uses to help us and thus to continue to manifest His love for us. The Bible Dictionary says that grace is "divine means of help or strength, given through the bounteous . . . love of Jesus Christ. . . . Grace is an *enabling power.*"[8] The Savior empowers us with His grace, not because we've earned it, but because He loves us perfectly. That is why grace is sweet. It was grace that I experienced at my father's bedside. It was grace that healed my friend from the horrors that haunted him after he had witnessed an unspeakable tragedy.

In the lyrics to his classic hymn "Amazing Grace," John Newton expressed a beautiful promise:

> *Through many dangers, toils and snares,*
> *I have already come;*
> *'Tis grace hath brought me safe thus far,*
> *And grace will lead me home.*[9]

THE SAVIOR EMPOWERS US WITH

HIS GRACE,

not because we've earned it, but

 BECAUSE

HE LOVES US

perfectly.

Grace is sweet.

I've never much cared for the word *sweet.* Unfortunately, I do love things that *taste* sweet. But the word *sweet* has always seemed a bit weak and even insipid. When I was a student at BYU, being called a "sweet spirit" was *not* considered a compliment. But I have come to understand that when we feel unexplainable peace or hope, love or strength, when we want to linger somewhere because the feeling is sweet, the Lord is manifesting His grace.

Years ago, I heard a woman I admire greatly say that when she saw the word *grace* in the scriptures, she substituted the word *power.*[10] More recently, Elder David A. Bednar suggested a similar approach: "In my personal scripture study, I often insert the term 'enabling power' whenever I encounter the word *grace.*"[11] This counsel helped me begin to make sense of many scriptures for the first time. *When we talk about the grace of Jesus Christ, we are talking about His power*—power that *enables* us to do things we simply could not do on our own.

The Savior has "all power" in heaven and on earth.[12] He has power to cleanse, forgive, and redeem us; power to heal us of weakness, sadness, illness, and heartache; power to inspire us; power to conquer Satan and overcome the flesh; power to work miracles; power to deliver us from circumstances we can't escape ourselves; power over death; and power to strengthen us. When the Apostle Paul said, "I can do all things through Christ which strengtheneth me,"[13] he was describing grace.

THIS POWER IS NEVER DORMANT.
IT IS NOT SUDDENLY UNLEASHED
WHEN WE SIN OR NEED HELP.

The flow of divine help is continuous, everywhere present, waiting for us to seek help. Elder Tad R. Callister explained that the powers of the Atonement "are always extending themselves, reaching out, penetrating every open heart. It is these powers that help fire the desire to repent. It is these powers that can inspire our course of conduct before sin is ever committed. . . . Suffice it to say, the Atonement is much more than a divine remedy to correct our sins after they are committed. The Atonement is, in fact, the most powerful motivational force in the world *to be good* from day to day and, when necessary, to repent when we have fallen short."[14] Because of the Atonement, as Elder Bruce C. Hafen explained, we may "learn from our experience without being condemned by that experience."[15] Thus, grace is divine power that enables us to handle things we can't figure out, can't do, can't overcome, or can't manage on our own. We have access to this power because Jesus Christ, who was already a God, condescended to endure the bitterness of a fallen world and experience *all* physical and spiritual pain.[16]

Elder David A. Bednar taught that "the Savior has suffered not just for our sins and iniquities—but also for our physical pains and anguish, our weaknesses and shortcomings, our fears and frustrations, our disappointments and discouragement, our regrets and remorse, our despair and desperation, the injustices and inequities we experience, and the emotional distresses that beset us. There is no physical pain, no spiritual wound, no anguish of soul or heartache, no infirmity or weakness you or I ever confront in mortality that the Savior did not experience first."[17]

BECAUSE JESUS CHRIST
ATONED, HIS GRACE IS AVAILABLE
TO US EVERY MINUTE OF EVERY
HOUR OF EVERY DAY.

It is this power that ultimately enables us to do what we came to earth to do. What is grace? Grace is divine enabling power.

WHAT DIFFERENCE CAN GRACE MAKE IN OUR LIVES?

N ot long ago I found myself facing a span of months that were going to be unusually intense. I had somehow managed to make more commitments than I could possibly handle during that period of time, and when I mapped out on paper all the things I'd committed to do, along with their deadlines, the task ahead looked impossible. I felt paralyzed about being able to follow through on everything I'd promised to do.

One Saturday, I worked all day trying to make a dent in looming deadlines before joining my family at the temple for a niece's endowment. As

I walked into the chapel and sat down, the tears started, and they would not stop. Exhaustion and the sheer fear of letting people down had me totally undone. But then I had one of those experiences you hear about in Sunday School. I picked up a copy of the Book of Mormon and flipped it open, only to have my eyes fall on this verse: "The Lord God showeth us our weakness that we may know that it is by *his* grace, and his great condescensions unto the children of men, that we have power to do these things."[18]

The word *weakness* stood out as though it were in neon because at the moment, I felt consumed by my weaknesses and inadequacies and utter fallibility. That verse led me to surrounding verses to understand the context of that promise. In short, what the Nephites in those verses had power to do was work miracles. Miracles! That was *exactly* what I needed, so I read on. Because of the Nephites' faith, they could command in the name of Jesus and the trees and mountains and waves of the sea would obey them.[19] My mind began to race over the countless times the

Lord had helped me in similarly stressful, difficult situations. Suddenly I felt a quiet surge of faith and a calming kind of reassurance that He would help me again. Tears flowed again, but this time with a sense of relief rather than sheer fear.

FAITH UNLOCKS DIVINE POWER,
AND FOR THE FIRST TIME IN WEEKS,
I FELT PEACE. PEACE FROM THE
PRINCE OF PEACE. IT WAS SWEET.

Not long ago, a friend was on the verge of resigning from a position of authority in a job he loved because working with a certain colleague had become so perpetually exasperating that he just didn't feel his paycheck was worth the daily agony. Then a curious set of circumstances unfolded in which my friend had the opportunity to become acquainted with his colleague's extended family. Somehow, that experience made all the difference, and in a way he couldn't quite explain, he better understood his colleague's heart and had new ideas about how to work with him. It was a sweet tender mercy.

The Lord's tender mercies come to those "whom he hath chosen, because of their faith, to make them mighty even unto the power of deliverance."[20]

TENDER MERCIES ARE ALWAYS
EVIDENCE THAT GRACE IS PRESENT.

In this case, the Lord's grace made manifest through a tender mercy delivered my friend from what had been daily agony at work. The circumstances didn't change, and the colleague who drove him crazy didn't change, but his ability to deal with his circumstances at work changed almost overnight.

We all know what it feels like to be overwhelmed with weaknesses, feelings, and circumstances we don't like and don't want—jealousy, fear, resentment, anger, anxiety, sadness, a lack of self-discipline, insecurity, and on and on. Mortality gives us a visceral experience with the

He rarely moves the

mountains in front of us,

—— BUT ——

He always helps us

CLIMB THEM.

reality that without the Lord, we are nothing.[21] If there are times when you think, "I can't handle for one more day my children, or my checkbook, or my job, or my illness, or the urge to eat brownies at midnight, or the lack of a spouse, or the lack of a *good* spouse, or a family who doesn't appreciate me," you're not alone. The Savior's divine empathy is perfect, so He knows how to help us.

He rarely moves the mountains in front of us, but He always helps us climb them.

Because of the Atonement of Jesus Christ and His grace, you don't have to confront fear, grief, insecurity, or an addiction alone. Because of Him, every one of us has the hope of a glorious future. Because of Him, we can have clean slates, second chances, new beginnings. Because of Him, everything is possible. Because of Him, we will never die.

With His help, you can resist temptation. With His help, you can forgive those who've hurt you and start over. With His help, you can leave your past behind. With His help, you can become your true self. With His help, your capacity and energy can increase. With His help, you can be happy again. With His help, as Sister Linda K. Burton taught, "all that is unfair about life can be made right through the Atonement of Jesus Christ."[22] The Savior promised, "My grace is sufficient for all men that humble themselves before me; for if they humble themselves before me, and have faith in me, then will I make weak things become strong unto them."[23] In short, with His help, we can change—truly change.

When the Savior is talking about "weak things," He is talking about us.

HIS GRACE CAN CHANGE OUR
VERY NATURE AND OVER TIME
TRANSFORM US FROM WHO WE ARE
INTO WHO WE CAN BECOME.

The Savior gives us access to God the Father and His power as well as to all of the gifts and blessings He wants to give His children. He pleads with us to "come boldly unto the throne of

23

grace, that we may obtain mercy, and find grace to help in time of need."[24] Likewise, Enoch was speaking to the Lord when he said, "Thou hast . . . given unto me a right to thy throne, and not of myself, but through thine own grace."[25]

We shouldn't treat or think about the Lord as we sometimes do about our visiting or home teachers when we're ill and could use some help— we hate to let them in to help us until we can solve our problems or clean the house first. If we think we have to conquer a bad habit or an addiction by ourselves, *before* we seek help, we most likely don't understand grace. If we're discouraged with ourselves because we feel weak and succumb too readily and too often to temptation, we don't understand grace. If our hearts are broken and we're dealing with waves of sadness because of something that has hurt us or someone we love, and we can't see our way to happiness again, we don't understand grace. If we keep trying to suppress envy or anger that rises up at the worst moments, if we feel as though nothing ever changes in our lives and we can't seem to get over unfairness or hurt, if we feel unworthy of the Lord's help, we don't understand grace. If the temple endowment remains a mystery and the power there has escaped us, if we don't know how to open the heavens and receive revelation, we don't understand grace.

IN OTHER WORDS, IF WE FEEL AS THOUGH WE'RE ALONE AND MUST RELY LARGELY OR EVEN SOLELY UPON OUR OWN ENERGY, TALENT, AND STRENGTH—WE DON'T UNDERSTAND GRACE.

Or, better said, we don't understand the enabling power of Jesus Christ.

Said Elder David A. Bednar: "Most of us clearly understand that the Atonement is for sinners. I am not so sure, however, that we know and understand that the Atonement is also for saints—for good men and women who are obedient and worthy and conscientious and who are striving to become better and serve more faithfully. I frankly do not think many of us 'get it' concerning this enabling and strengthening aspect of the Atonement, and I wonder if we mistakenly believe we must make the journey from good to better and become a saint all by ourselves through sheer grit, willpower, and discipline, and with our obviously limited capacities."[26] I love the account of Enoch, which surely helps bolster the hope and confidence of every person who has ever received an assignment or responsibility that overwhelmed him or her. In other words, every one of us. When the Lord spoke from heaven and charged Enoch with preaching repentance to his people, Enoch was stunned, saying, in essence, "You must be kidding! I'm just a boy and the people don't even like me because 'I am slow of speech; wherefore am I thy servant?'"[27]

The Lord's response was reassuring while also being to the point: Just "go forth and do as I have commanded thee, and no man shall pierce thee. Open thy mouth, and it shall be filled."[28] Enoch may not have had much if any confidence, but

Faith
IN THE LORD
AND IN HIS GRACE,
coupled with obedience
and earnest seeking,
CAN LITERALLY TURN
WEAKNESS INTO
STRENGTH.

he did have faith—faith enough to attempt to do what the Lord had asked him to do.

As a result of Enoch's faith, the Lord didn't just bless him and help him accomplish a mighty task. He turned his weakness into a strength: "So great was the faith of Enoch that . . . he spake the word of the Lord, and the earth trembled, and the mountains fled, even according to his command; and the rivers of water were turned out of their course . . . and all nations feared greatly, so powerful was the word of Enoch, and so great was the power of the language which God had given him."[29]

Faith in the Lord and in His grace, coupled with obedience and earnest seeking, can literally turn weakness into strength.

During one particularly difficult season of life, I was fighting off waves of melancholy one Sunday afternoon when I drove to the Jordan River Temple, pulled into the parking lot, and opened my scriptures to look for solace. I vividly remember turning to a scripture I had read countless times before: "And if men come unto me I will show unto them their weakness. I give unto men weakness that they may be humble; and my grace is sufficient for all men that humble themselves before me; for if they humble themselves before me, and have faith in me, then will I make weak things become strong unto them."[30]

In that moment, the words *weakness, grace,* and *become strong* jumped off the page. Even more, the Spirit somehow communicated to my heart and mind that in that verse lay the answer to the pain and heartache with which I was wrestling. I felt, perhaps for the first time, that I wasn't expected to "handle" this challenge alone. I didn't really know what that meant, but over time I would begin to learn that

THE LORD HAD ALREADY PAID
THE PRICE FOR MY PAIN.

If I would humble myself and believe in His power to help me, He would turn this time of weakness into a season of healing and growth. It wasn't magic, and relief wasn't instantaneous, but that moment in a temple parking lot proved to be a turning point in my life. It was the beginning of a major shift in both my attitude and my understanding. Many times since then, I have thanked the Lord for the gift of that painful season of life that drove me to the scriptures to find answers and comfort.

What difference can grace make in the lives of sincere people? For those who seek to understand the Lord's infinite capacity to help us through His infinite and eternal Atonement, it can make *all* the difference!

How does the Savior make His power available to us?

Elder Bruce R. McConkie said that "if it were not for the grace of God, there would be nothing—no creation, no fall, no mortal probation, no atonement, no redemption, no immortality, no eternal life. It is God's grace that underlies all things, [and] . . . that makes all things possible. Without it there would be nothing; with it there is everything."[31]

Elder Jeffrey R. Holland added further clarity: "Much of the miraculous help we find in the gospel is just that—a miracle from heaven, the power of divine priesthood, the attendance of angels administering to us through a very thin veil.

These are gifts from God, manifestations of His grace."[32]

EVERY DIVINE GIFT AND EVERY
SPIRITUAL PRIVILEGE THAT GIVES US
ACCESS TO THE POWER OF HEAVEN
COMES FROM CHRIST OR THROUGH
CHRIST OR BECAUSE OF CHRIST,
THROUGH HIS GRACE.

We owe *everything* to Him and our Father in Heaven, including the privileges of receiving the gift and power of the Holy Ghost; of receiving personal revelation and gifts of the Spirit; of being endowed in the temple with knowledge and priesthood power; of learning the "mysteries of the kingdom, even the key of the knowledge of God";[33] of having angels on our right and on our left;[34] of receiving all the blessings of the Atonement; and of receiving eternal life, the "greatest of all the gifts of God."[35] We owe every divine gift and all access to divine power to the grace of Jesus Christ.

The grace of Jesus Christ gives Latter-day Saints, both men and women, access to the gift and power of the Holy Ghost, to the ministering of angels, and to countless gifts of the Spirit, just to name a few.[36] No wonder Eliza R. Snow said that Latter-day Saint women "have greater and higher privileges than any other females upon the face of the earth."[37] I stand with Eliza on this.

But there is one privilege that latter-day women in particular likely overlook—the privilege of having access to priesthood power.[38] Too many sisters *as well as* priesthood bearers think LDS women don't have this privilege. *But that is not true.* Women who have been endowed in the temple have *as much access* to priesthood power *for their own lives* as do ordained men.

Four key points underscore this truth: First, priesthood keys are the manner through which the Lord authorizes the use of and distributes His power, *for both women and men.*

Second, there are distinctions between

priesthood keys, priesthood authority, and priesthood power. Priesthood keys are required to authorize ordinances, priesthood authority is required to perform ordinances, and priesthood power is available to all who worthily receive ordinances and keep the associated covenants.

Third, both men and women who serve under the direction of priesthood keys serve with divine authority.[39] Elder Dallin H. Oaks explained: "We are not accustomed to speaking of women having the authority of the priesthood in their Church callings, *but what other authority can it be?* When a woman—young or old—is set apart to preach the gospel as a full-time missionary, she is given priesthood authority to perform a priesthood function. The same is true when a woman is set apart to function as an officer or teacher in a Church organization under the direction of one who holds the keys of the priesthood. Whoever functions in an office or calling received from one who holds priesthood keys exercises priesthood authority in performing her or his assigned duties."[40]

And finally, fourth, men and women have equal access to the Lord's highest spiritual privileges. Nowhere is this more apparent than in the house of the Lord. Elder M. Russell Ballard declared that "when men and women go to the temple, they are both endowed with the same power, which by definition is priesthood power. . . . Access to the power and the blessings of the priesthood is available to all of God's children."[41]

THOUGH WOMEN ARE NOT ORDAINED TO OFFICES IN THE PRIESTHOOD, IN THE TEMPLE THEY ARE ENDOWED WITH PRIESTHOOD POWER AND WITH KNOWLEDGE OF HOW TO USE THAT POWER.[42]

There are those who wonder why women are not eligible for priesthood ordination. But the better question is: Why is it not necessary for women to be ordained? The impact of this question is perhaps best illustrated when considering the requirements to enter the temple. Both men and women must meet certain worthiness requirements to enter the house of the Lord. These requirements are exactly the same—with one major exception. When a woman meets those requirements, she is authorized by priesthood leaders who have keys to attend the temple. But meeting worthiness requirements is not enough for a male; a man must also be ordained. A woman needs no priesthood ordination to receive the blessings of the temple—this despite the fact that all ordinances in the temple are priesthood ordinances, that all who enter the temple officiate in priesthood ordinances, that all who are endowed in the temple wear the garment of the holy priesthood, and that all who participate in the endowment don other pieces of sacred clothing, including the robes of the holy priesthood. So again, why is a woman not required to be ordained to participate in the highest ordinances of the priesthood in the very same way men participate inside the temple, the holiest place on earth? We don't have an answer for that question either, but surely this isn't just an oversight on the part of the Lord.

IN SHORT, WHEN ALL IS SAID
AND DONE, NEITHER COVENANT
WOMEN NOR MEN EVER LACK
FOR DIVINE AUTHORITY.

Further, God's highest ordinances are available only to a man and woman together. In this single doctrinal provision, God indicates His profound respect for the distinctive but vitally interconnected roles of both men and women. Said Elder David A. Bednar: "The unique combination of spiritual, physical, mental, and emotional capacities of both males and females was needed to enact the plan of happiness. . . . The man and the woman are intended to learn from, strengthen, bless, and complete each other."[43] This reality is demonstrated nowhere more compellingly than in the temple, where the highest priesthood ordinances available on earth are

THROUGH

HIS GRACE,

He has made His highest,

HOLIEST SPIRITUAL PRIVILEGES

available to both

MEN AND WOMEN.

available only to a man and woman together. Neither men nor women have an edge when it comes to qualifying for exaltation.

And finally, women have claim to *all blessings* that emanate from the priesthood. Again from Elder McConkie: "Where spiritual things are concerned, as pertaining to all of the gifts of the Spirit, with reference to the receipt of revelation, the gaining of testimonies, and the seeing of visions, in all matters that pertain to godliness and holiness . . . in all these things men and women stand in a position of absolute equality before the Lord."[44]

We may not presently have the answers to all questions. But we do know, as Lehi told his son Jacob, that "all things have been done in the wisdom of him who knoweth all things."[45]

Most important, we live in the dispensation of the fulness of times, when no spiritual blessings are being withheld from the earth.[46] No men or women living *anytime, anywhere* have had greater access to divine power than we do. If we seek for a lifetime, we won't plumb the depth of power and breadth of spiritual privileges the Lord has given us. Through His grace, He has made His highest, holiest spiritual privileges available to both men and women. *That* is our doctrine. *That* is the truth.

WHAT MUST WE DO TO GAIN ACCESS TO THE SAVIOR'S POWER?

I recently visited Harvard University and honestly felt a little smarter just walking across campus. But later that day, I went to the Boston Temple, and the contrast between one of the world's most elite universities and the Lord's house, which is *the* institution of highest learning, was striking. Everything felt different! The world's finest education simply pales when compared with the tutelage of God and the education He is willing to give those who seek after Him.[47] Even an Ivy League institution can't compete with the "wonders of eternity" and "hidden mysteries" from the Lord's kingdom throughout the ages.[48]

Elder Dallin H. Oaks said that "in contrast to the institutions of the world, which teach us to *know* something, the gospel of Jesus Christ challenges us to *become* something."[49]

OUR ACCESS TO DIVINE
POWER HINGES UPON WHO
WE ARE BECOMING.

I doubt we quote any scripture on grace more often than Nephi's, that "it is by grace that we are saved, after all we can do."[50] As covenant men and women, we have a tendency to zoom in on the "*after* all *we* can do" part of the grace-and-works equation, but then wonder how we can possibly do more than we already are—though we're pretty sure whatever we're doing isn't enough.

The very idea of "after all we can do" can easily trip us up. None of us are capable of doing our very best work or being our very best selves or giving our very best effort constantly, without variation. We're mortals, dealing with the drag of the natural man, and from day to day our best efforts vary. But the Savior knew this before He atoned, and He certainly understands it now, because He felt all of it as He bore the incomprehensible weight and pain of our burdens, our inadequacies, and our weaknesses—in addition to our sins and mistakes.

Both our Father and His Son understood that in a fallen world, we would sin and make mistakes, some of them over and over again. We would get tired, be sad, lose our patience, hurt each other, get enamored with the superficiality of the world, succumb to pride, and basically have to engage in an exhausting, unrelenting kind of hand-to-hand combat with the natural man.

"After all we can do" is not about sequence or timing, nor is it about feverishly working our way through an exhaustive list of good works. Elder Bruce C. Hafen wrote that "the Savior's gift of grace to us is not necessarily limited in time to 'after' all we can do. We may receive His grace before, during, and after the time when we expend our own efforts."[51]

"After all we can do" is also not about a to-do

list. It has very little to do with quantity or output. Jesus Christ is the only one to ever walk this earth who did all that could be done in mortality.

Instead, doing all we can do is about the direction we're headed and what kind of men and women we are becoming. There is nothing simple about this, because it isn't natural for the natural man or woman to want to do good or be good. Referring to a statement by President Spencer W. Kimball, Elder Oaks has said that "the repenting sinner must suffer for his sins, but this suffering has a different purpose than punishment or payment. Its purpose is *change*."[52]

Jesus Christ endured and completed His eternal, infinite Atonement so that you and I could change. So that we wouldn't be tripped up by our sins or nagging weaknesses and doomed eternally. So that we wouldn't have to pay for our sins forever, the price of which none of us has the capacity to pay. So that we could keep learning and practicing being Saints—realizing that practice *always* involves mistakes. The Lord has made it clear that no unclean thing can dwell with Him,[53]

JESUS CHRIST

endured and completed His eternal,

INFINITE ATONEMENT

——— SO THAT ———

you and I could change.

but it is equally clear that no unclean person, meaning no unchanged person, will even want to.

Harvard Business School professor Clayton Christensen tells about a young adult man who, in a sacrament meeting address, said this about repentance: "We often view repentance as a slow process. It isn't. Change is instantaneous. It is *not changing* that takes so much time."[54]

> A TRUE, ENDURING TRANSFORMATION OF THE HEART THAT LEADS TO PERMANENT CHANGE ISN'T POSSIBLE ON OUR OWN.

We can't will it or gut it out through some kind of clenched-teeth self-discipline. But neither is it possible without our sincere, sustained effort, as Elder D. Todd Christofferson explained: "Through the Atonement of Jesus Christ and His grace, our failures to live the celestial law perfectly and consistently in mortality can be erased and we are enabled to develop a Christlike character.

46

Justice demands, however, that none of this happen without our willing agreement and participation. It has ever been so. Our very presence on earth as physical beings is the consequence of a choice each of us made to participate in our Father's plan. Thus, salvation is certainly not the result of divine whim, but neither does it happen by divine will alone."[55]

Thus, if we are willing to yield to "the enticings of the Holy Spirit," to stay on the covenant path, to hold tightly to the iron rod, and to partake of the fruit again and again, it is possible to put "off the natural man and [become] a saint through the atonement of Christ"[56] and be transformed from fallen men and women riddled with faults into true disciples.

"DOING ALL WE CAN DO"
IS ALL ABOUT DISCIPLESHIP.

Discipleship requires at least three things of us: first, coming to love the Lord more than we love anything in the world; second, experiencing a change of heart so that we have no "disposition to do evil, but to do good continually"[57]—which doesn't mean we no longer make mistakes, it just means we don't want to; and third, behaving like true followers.

The road to discipleship leads away from all forms of ungodliness.[58] That means resisting the gravitational pull of the world and shedding the attitudes, appetites, and behaviors of the natural man or woman. As Elder Neal A. Maxwell put it, "Personal sacrifice never was placing an animal on the altar. Instead, it is a willingness to put the animal in us upon the altar."[59]

AT THE HEART OF BECOMING DISCIPLES IS DOING WHAT WE PROMISE TO DO EVERY TIME WE PARTAKE OF THE SACRAMENT—WHICH IS TO "ALWAYS REMEMBER" THE LORD.[60]

This means remembering Him when we choose what media we're willing to expose our spirits to. It means remembering Him in how we spend our time and when choosing between a steady diet of pop culture or the word of God. It means remembering Him in the middle of conflict or when temptation looms. It means remembering Him when sincere questions arise about the Church or the gospel, questions that deserve pondering and contemplation in an environment of faith rather than doubt. It means remembering Him every time we partake of an ordinance, because every ordinance points to Him. It means remembering Him Monday through Saturday as well as Sunday. It means remembering Him when critics attack His Church and mock truth, which will likely happen more and more often in future days. It means remembering that we have taken His name upon us.[61] And it means working at being obedient.

Elder Jeffrey R. Holland put our challenge this way: "Through all our trials in life we must truly strive to be righteous. We may not ever be free from pain. We certainly won't be free from problems. We won't always have bright, sunny days. Sometimes money, talent, opportunity, and tempers will be short. . . . But through all this we can be righteous! . . . We know we can't escape trouble, but we should do everything humanly possible to escape sin."[62]

Because we are mortals, and mortals by definition make mistakes, our discipleship and our access to the Lord's grace depend upon our willingness to repent, as Elder D. Todd Christofferson explained: "Christ died not to save indiscriminately but to offer repentance. We rely 'wholly upon the merits of him who is mighty to save' in the process of repentance, but acting to repent is a self-willed change. So by making repentance a condition for receiving the gift of grace, God enables us to retain responsibility for ourselves. Repentance respects and sustains our moral agency."[63]

None of us are perfectly obedient—not yet. Perhaps none of us have mastered the process of *always* completely, fully repenting or completely, fully taking the Lord's name upon us. But it is our quest, because conversion to the Lord requires immersion in His gospel. We baptize by immersion, not by sprinkling.

A "SPRINKLING" OF THE GOSPEL WILL NEVER LEAD TO CONVERSION.

If we constantly immerse ourselves in a fallen world, how far can we really expect to progress in this life? I am not suggesting that there aren't fun and even inspiring opportunities all around us. I love ball games and four-wheelers and travel and snowshoeing and Broadway plays with the best of them. But mortality is a short-term proposition.[64] None of us will stay here long. Doesn't it make sense to devote as much energy as possible to things we can actually take with us into the eternities? To covenants, eternal relationships, our knowledge of truth, and the blessings that come from devotion to the Lord? And those blessings are remarkable.

Elder Christofferson related an experience of two sister missionaries serving in Croatia who were headed home late one evening after an appointment. He told the story this way: "Several men on the trolley made crude comments and became rather menacing. Feeling threatened, the sisters got off the trolley at the next stop just as the doors closed so no one could follow them. Having avoided that problem, they realized they were in a place unknown to either of them. As they turned to look for help, they saw a woman. . . . She knew where they could find another trolley to take them home and invited them to follow her. On the way they had to pass a bar with patrons sitting along the sidewalk. . . . These men also appeared threatening. Nevertheless, the two young women had the distinct impression that the men could not see them. They walked by, apparently invisible to [the men]. . . . When the sisters and their guide reached the stop, the trolley they needed was just arriving. They turned to thank the woman, but she was nowhere to be seen."[65] How are we to explain this sequence of events? The discipleship of two sister missionaries gave them access to the Lord's protecting grace.

Discipleship is not easy, but it is easier than

WHEN WE TURN OUR LIVES OVER TO THE LORD,

the power behind us

—— is always greater than the ——

OBSTACLES BEFORE US.

not becoming a disciple. Paraphrasing President Howard W. Hunter: If our lives are centered on Christ, nothing can ever go permanently wrong. But if they're not centered on Christ, nothing can ever go permanently right.[66]

Elder Dallin H. Oaks has taught that "when you're involved in the work of the Lord, the power behind you is always greater than the obstacles before you."[67] We might also say that when we turn our lives over to the Lord, the power behind us is always greater than the obstacles before us. That does not mean we won't have problems. It doesn't mean we'll never have disappointments. It doesn't mean we'll never have our hearts broken or be mistreated or lose our jobs without cause or face challenges that seem to have no solution. In fact, we can almost count on the fact that we'll face challenges bigger than we are.

But Nephi saw our day and what we would face, and he expressed in his language what Elder Oaks taught. Nephi "beheld the power of the Lamb of God, that it descended upon the saints of the church of the Lamb, and upon the covenant people of the Lord, who were scattered upon all the face of the earth; and they were armed with righteousness and with the power of God in great glory."[68]

TRUE DISCIPLES ARE ARMED WITH RIGHTEOUSNESS, MEANING WITH BOTH DELIVERANCE AND DIVINE PROTECTION, AND WITH THE POWER OF GOD IN GREAT GLORY.

This means that, as disciples, imperfect though we still are, we can ask for more energy, more revelation, more patience, more self-discipline, more hope, more love, more healing, more happiness. We can ask for miracles, for freedom from pain, and for the desire to forgive. We can ask for more faith and for help in becoming better disciples.[69] We can ask for angels to walk with us, because if we live up to our privileges, angels can't be restrained from being our associates.[70] And we can also ask for help to understand why the Lord sometimes responds to our requests and at other times manifests His grace in our lives differently than we may have hoped. The Lord's timing and His wisdom about what we need at any given point in our lives reigns supreme.

Nonetheless, the Lord is not saving up His grace or power for one dramatic display at the Final Judgment, nor is grace something that kicks in at the end of an ordeal. *It is there from the moment we exercise even a "particle of faith" and ask for His help.*[71] Jesus Christ is Alpha and Omega, literally the beginning and the end,[72] which means He'll stick with us from start to finish.

Not long ago, I was assigned to make a sensitive presentation to a group of senior General Authorities. That kind of assignment is always a little nerve-wracking. I prepared the best I could and sought the Lord's help, even asking if angels could accompany me to the meeting. Things went better that day than I expected—which should have tipped me off. As I walked back to my office thinking, "That went pretty well," I had an immediate and very clear impression, "You

don't think *you're* the one who did that, do you?"
In a moment I realized that the Lord had indeed
sent help. When all is said and done, anything we
do well is a gift from God.

I can't think of a single thing I've ever been
asked to do that I've been equal to. But therein
lies the beautiful intersection of grace and works.

WHEN DISCIPLES DO
THEIR BEST, WHATEVER THAT
IS AT A GIVEN MOMENT,
THE LORD MAGNIFIES US.

Doing all we can do is about becoming and
behaving like true disciples of the Lord Jesus
Christ. That is our part.

As Elder Neal A. Maxwell put it: "Many on
this planet hunger for bread, but many also hunger deeply to experience the reassuring eloquence
of example. This represents a desperate need that
is incumbent upon us to provide as part of our
discipleship."[73]

That being said, make no mistake about it: *notwithstanding* all we can do and *despite* the little we actually do, it is the Savior's grace that will ultimately save us.[74] We can never earn exaltation. But we can indicate by the choices we make and the way we live our lives that

WE WANT TO BE PART OF THE

KINGDOM OF GOD MORE THAN

WE WANT ANYTHING ELSE.

And that is discipleship.

So where do we go from here? During one mission president training seminar, Elder Jeffrey R. Holland encouraged new mission presidents to "have an eternal love affair with the life of the Son of God. I pray that you will . . . love everything He did, everywhere He went, everything He said, and everything He is. I would walk on hot lava, I would drink broken glass to find one more word, one more phrase, one more doctrine, *any* parable that *anyone* could give me of the life of Christ the living Son of the living God. The doctrine of

Christ means everything to me as a result of [my feelings] for the author of the doctrine of Christ."[75]

What one thing would you be willing to give up, starting today, to have that kind of feeling about the Savior and to put Him even more at the center of your life? What one thing would you be willing to start doing or stop doing? What one thing would you be willing to do, starting today, to unlock more of His power? Four decades ago, President Spencer W. Kimball declared, "I can see no good reason why the Lord would open doors that we are not prepared to enter."[76] Surely that statement, and the meaning behind it, applies not only to the Church as an organization but to each of us in our personal spiritual growth and development. It is learning how to gain access to the Savior's grace that will enable us to do what He is counting on us to do in the twilight of this great, culminating gospel dispensation.

Elder Holland put the task before us in perspective: "Something is going to be asked of this dispensation that's never been asked before. . . . [We] must be ready to present the Church of the

Lamb, to the Lamb, and when that happens, we must be looking and acting like His Church."[77] Indeed, the Lord is hastening His work, and we are right in the middle of the hastening. I loved it when a sister opened a Relief Society meeting in Houston by praying, "We are grateful to live in this day when we are preparing the world for the return of Jesus Christ."

Think of it! The eyes and hopes of every previous dispensation are upon us. We've been chosen to help prepare the world for the Savior. We are living in a day unlike any other, which means *it is time for us to do things we have never done before.*

Because we are disciples of Christ, how will we make sure that we and our loved ones are converted? Because we're disciples of Christ, what will we never do or even tolerate again? Because we're disciples of Christ, what truths are we willing to stand for, even if they aren't popular? Because we're disciples of Christ, how will we treat those who see the world, and even the Church, differently? Because we're disciples of Christ, what are *we* willing to do to *build up* the kingdom of

We are living in a day unlike any other,

— WHICH MEANS —

IT IS TIME FOR US
TO DO THINGS

we have never done before.

God?[78] Because we're disciples of Christ, how hard will we work to unlock the Savior's power?

THE MORE WE UNLOCK THE POWER AVAILABLE TO US AS COVENANT-MAKING MEN AND WOMEN, THE MORE VIBRANT OUR IMPACT WILL BE IN THE WORK OF SALVATION.

We will receive more revelation more often; we will learn to utilize the power we've been endowed with; we will perform more temple work and worship; our families will be more centered on Christ and more eager to share the gospel; and we will have more righteous influence. Period.

The key to unlocking the power of covenant men and women is in covenant men's and women's learning to unlock the power of Jesus Christ.

I know how tangible the Lord's power is. I was in my early thirties when an opportunity to marry evaporated overnight and the heartache plunged me into depression. One day a friend called to say she'd had an impression that a verse in Mosiah was just for me, and then she read the verse over the phone: "I will also ease the burdens which are put upon your shoulders, that even you cannot feel them upon your backs, even while you are in bondage; and this will I do that ye may stand as witnesses for me hereafter, and that ye may know of a surety that I, the Lord God, do visit my people in their afflictions."[79]

I'm sorry to say that I hung up even more discouraged. As foolish as it sounds now, I wasn't looking for the Lord to ease my burdens—I just wanted Him to send my husband! I felt I couldn't face the burden of singleness *one more day.* I was sure that if I prayed and fasted and went to the temple enough, I could convince Him to bless me with this righteous desire. I wasn't thinking about standing as a witness. I was far too preoccupied with myself—which is what happens when we try to lift our burdens alone.

Weeks stretched into a year, and with all of my praying and fasting and temple-going, I was still single and still miserable. But then one day

I noticed a verse in the book of Luke in which the Savior declares that He has come to heal the brokenhearted.[80] The word *brokenhearted* leaped off the page, because my heart had been broken. I was still thinking about that verse a few days later when I found myself meeting with Elder Bruce C. Hafen about a manuscript he had written on the enabling power of the Atonement. I took that manuscript home and devoured every word. It opened my eyes to scriptures and divine promises I had never seen before: that the Lord would heal our wounded souls, that He had already taken our pains upon Him, and that He would succor us.[81] I realized then that I didn't know very much about the Savior.

AND IT SIMPLY ISN'T POSSIBLE
TO BE A DISCIPLE OF SOMEONE
YOU DON'T KNOW.

Fast-forward thirty years. In some respects, my life hasn't changed much. But in other ways, *everything* is different. That painful episode was a vital turning point, because it launched me on a continuing quest to understand the Atonement and the power that flows from it. Life would have crushed me long ago if I hadn't learned how to access the Savior's power. He has carried me and healed my heart again and again.

As I prepared the address on grace that I mentioned at the outset, I had yet another personal, tangible experience with the power and the grace of Jesus Christ. Just five days before I was to deliver that message, I suddenly became very ill—perhaps more ill than I had ever been—and by the time I could see my doctor, I was one sick person. He took one look at me, ran some tests, told me how seriously ill I was, and even threatened me with going to the hospital. He then told me it would take at least ten days to get me back on my feet. I said, "Well, that's fine, but I have one tiny problem. Less than three days from now, I need to be able to stand at a pulpit for thirty-five minutes and talk to about fifteen thousand of my best friends." He looked at me as though every marble had rolled out of my head and then went to work to do everything he could medically to help me.

At the appointed hour, I stood at the pulpit and with a raspy voice that gave out at times nonetheless fulfilled that obligation. It wouldn't have happened without the care of my superb physician, but when all is said and done, that was not the deciding factor. It was the prayers and fasting of family and friends. It was help from the other side of the veil.

> PRIESTHOOD POWER IS REAL.
> ANGELS REALLY DO MINISTER
> THROUGH A VERY THIN VEIL.

Fasting and prayer truly do give us access to the power of God and to manifestations of the grace of Jesus Christ.

President Gordon B. Hinckley put in perspective the stunning nature of what the Savior did for us: "I sense in a measure the meaning of His Atonement. I cannot comprehend it all. It is so vast in its reach and yet so intimate in its effect

The path of

DISCIPLESHIP

IS ACTUALLY THE EASIEST PATH.

It is the path that allows us

to partake most fully of

THE LORD'S LOVE

FOR US.

that it defies comprehension. When all is said and done, when all of history is examined, when the deepest depths of the human mind have been explored, there is nothing so wonderful, so majestic, so tremendous as this act of grace when the Son of the Almighty, the prince of His Father's royal household, . . . gave His life in ignominy and pain so that all of the sons and daughters of God, of all generations of time, every one of whom must die, might walk again and live eternally."[82]

ULTIMATELY, FOR EVERY ONE OF US, THE SAVIOR IS OUR ONLY CHANCE.

Our only chance to overcome self-doubt and catch a vision of who we may become. Our only chance to repent and have our sins washed away. Our only chance to purify our hearts, subdue our weaknesses, and avoid the adversary. Our only chance to obtain redemption and exaltation. Our only chance to find peace and happiness in this life and eternal life in the world to come.

The Lord knows the way because He is the

way. He is our only chance for successfully negotiating mortality. His Atonement makes available all of the power, peace, light, and strength that we need to deal with life's challenges.

I do stand all amazed at the love Jesus offers us. And I also stand as a witness that the Lord's grace is real and that He visits His people in their afflictions, in their weaknesses, and in their infirmities. The Savior really is filled with healing, enabling power, and He can ease our burdens and strengthen us when we feel weaker than weak. That is why the path of discipleship is actually the easiest path. It is the path that allows us to partake most fully of the Lord's love for us, which has no end—which is why the fruit of the tree is sweet above all that is sweet.

This really is The Church of Jesus Christ of Latter-day Saints. Jesus Christ really *is* going to come again. Every knee really is going to bow and every tongue confess that He is the Christ. I know these things are true. May we be determined to unlock His power to help us be the disciples we want to be.

NOTES

1. See Isaiah 61:3.
2. See Linda K. Burton, "Wanted: Hands and Hearts to Hasten the Work"; Bonnie L. Oscarson, "Sisterhood: Oh, How We Need Each Other"; and Rosemary M. Wixom, "Keeping Covenants Protects Us, Prepares Us, and Empowers Us," *Ensign*, May 2014.
3. See 1 Nephi 8:18, 23, 28.
4. 1 Nephi 8:33.
5. 1 Nephi 8:12.
6. Alma 32:42.
7. 1 Nephi 11:22.
8. Bible Dictionary, s.v. "Grace," 697.
9. John Newton, "Amazing Grace," 1779.
10. More recently, Elder David A. Bednar has suggested the same approach (see David A. Bednar, "In the Strength of the Lord," BYU Devotional Address, 23 October 2001).
11. David A. Bednar, "The Atonement and the Journey of Mortality," *Ensign*, April 2012.

12. After His Resurrection, He declared to His remaining eleven Apostles, "*All power* is given unto me in heaven and in earth" (Matthew 28:18; emphasis added). John later bore record that the Savior "received a fulness of the glory of the Father" (D&C 93:16). See also Mosiah 4:9.
13. Philippians 4:13.
14. Tad R. Callister, *The Infinite Atonement* (2000), 212.
15. Bruce C. Hafen, "Eve Heard All These Things and Was Glad," in *Women in the Covenant of Grace,* ed. Dawn Hall Fletcher and Susan Fletcher Green (1994), 32.
16. Paul taught the Hebrews, "We have not an high priest which cannot be touched with the feeling of our infirmities; but was in all points tempted like as we are, yet without sin. Let us therefore come boldly unto the throne of grace, that we may obtain mercy, and find grace to help in time of need" (Hebrews 4:15–16).
17. David A. Bednar, "Bear Up Their Burdens with Ease," *Ensign,* May 2014.
18. Jacob 4:7.
19. See Jacob 4:6.
20. 1 Nephi 1:20.
21. See Alma 26:12. The statement about mortality giving us a "visceral experience" with the reality that, without the Lord, we are nothing originated with Wendy Watson Nelson.
22. Linda K. Burton, "Is Faith in the Atonement of Jesus Christ Written in Our Hearts?" *Ensign,* November 2012.
23. Ether 12:27.
24. Hebrews 4:16.
25. Moses 7:59.
26. Bednar, "In the Strength of the Lord," BYU Devotional, 23 October 2001.
27. Moses 6:31.
28. Moses 6:32.

29. Moses 7:13.

30. Ether 12:27.

31. Bruce R. McConkie, *A New Witness for the Articles of Faith* (1985), 149.

32. Jeffrey R. Holland, *For Times of Trouble* (2013). (Psalms 18:36; 94:18–29.)

33. D&C 84:19.

34. D&C 84:88.

35. D&C 14:7.

36. The Holy Ghost is one such avenue. Elder Parley P. Pratt described the breadth of the Holy Ghost's influence upon us: "The gift of the Holy Ghost . . . quickens all the intellectual faculties, increases, enlarges, expands, and purifies all the natural passions and affections. . . . It inspires, develops, cultivates, and matures all the fine-toned sympathies, joys, tastes, kindred feelings, and affections of our nature. It inspires virtue, kindness, goodness, tenderness, gentleness, and charity. It develops beauty of person, form, and features. . . . It strengthens and gives tone to the nerves. In short, it is, as it were, marrow to the bone, joy to the heart, light to the eyes, music to the ears, and life to the whole being" (Parley P. Pratt, *Key to the Science of Theology and a Voice of Warning* [2002], 61).

37. Eliza R. Snow, in *Evening News,* 14 January 1870.

38. Elder Bruce R. McConkie said that the "doctrine of the priesthood—unknown in the world and but little known even in the Church—cannot be learned out of the scriptures alone. . . . The doctrine of the priesthood is known only by personal revelation" ("The Doctrine of the Priesthood," *Ensign,* May 1982, 32).

39. See Sheri Dew, *Women and the Priesthood* (2013), especially chapter 6.

40. Dallin H. Oaks, "The Keys and Authority of the Priesthood," *Ensign,* May 2014; emphasis added.

41. M. Russell Ballard, "Let Us Think Straight," BYU Campus

Education Week Devotional Address, 20 August 2013; see also *New Era,* April 2014; D&C 109:15, 22. Elder D. Todd Christofferson taught that "in all the ordinances, especially those of the temple, we are endowed with power from on high" ("The Power of Covenants," *Ensign,* May 2009, 20, 22).

42. In the temple, we may "grow up" in the Lord, receive a "fulness of the Holy Ghost," and be armed with God's power (D&C 109:15, 22).

43. David A. Bednar, "We Believe in Being Chaste," *Ensign,* May 2013.

44. Bruce R. McConkie, "Our Sisters from the Beginning," *Ensign,* January 1979.

45. 2 Nephi 2:24.

46. See D&C 121:27–29.

47. See D&C 76:7–10.

48. D&C 76:7, 8.

49. Dallin H. Oaks, "The Challenge to Become," *Ensign,* November 2000.

50. 2 Nephi 25:23.

51. Bruce C. Hafen, *The Broken Heart* (1989), 155–56.

52. Dallin H. Oaks, *The Lord's Way* (1991), 223.

53. See Alma 40:26.

54. See "Why I Belong, and Why I Believe," Mormonism 101 Lecture, Harvard Law School.

55. D. Todd Christofferson, "Free Forever, to Act for Themselves," *Ensign,* November 2014.

56. Mosiah 3:19.

57. See Mosiah 5, especially Mosiah 5:2.

58. Moroni 10:32.

59. Neal A. Maxwell, "'Deny Yourselves of All Ungodliness,'" *Ensign,* May 1995.

60. See Moroni 4:3; 5:2.

61. See Mosiah 5:7.

62. Holland, *For Times of Trouble,* Psalms 145:14; 146:8.

63. Christofferson, "Free Forever."

64. Cicero purportedly said, "I am more interested in the long hereafter than in the brief present" (quoted by LeGrand Richards, "I Am More Interested in the Long Hereafter than in the Brief Present," BYU Devotional Address, 25 February 1975).

65. See D. Todd Christofferson, "When Thou Art Converted," *Ensign,* May 2004.

66. See Howard W. Hunter, "Fear Not, Little Flock," *1988–89 Devotional and Fireside Speeches* (1989), 112.

67. See "Hastening the Work in Europe," video on www.lds.org.

68. 1 Nephi 14:14.

69. Elder Marvin J. Ashton taught that there are "less-conspicuous gifts," such as the gift of being a disciple, the gift to calm, the gift of being agreeable, and so on ("'There Are Many Gifts,'" *Ensign,* November 1987).

70. See Minutes of the Nauvoo Female Relief Society, April 28, 1842.

71. See Alma 32:27.

72. See Revelation 1:8, 11; 21:6; 22:13; 3 Nephi 9:18; D&C 35:1; 45:7.

73. Neal A. Maxwell, "The Pathway of Discipleship," Church Educational System Fireside, 4 January 1998.

74. See 2 Nephi 10:24.

75. Jeffrey R. Holland, 2013 New Mission Presidents' Seminar.

76. Spencer W. Kimball, "When the World Will Be Converted," *Ensign,* October 1974.

77. Jeffrey R. Holland, in *Church News,* 17 February 2007.

78. See JST, Matthew 6:38.

79. Mosiah 24:14.

80. Luke 4:18.

81. See Luke 4:18; Alma 7:11–12; Jacob 2:8.

82. *Teachings of Gordon B. Hinckley* (1997), 28.